D1518673

The Supreme Court

by Karen Latchana Kenney

Consultant: John Coleman
Professor of Political Science, University of Minnesota
Minneapolis, Minnesota

BEARPORT
PUBLISHING

Minneapolis, Minnesota

Credits

Cover and Title Page, © OlegAlbinsky/iStock; 3, © Dan Thornberg/Shutterstock; 5, © John Gomez/ Shutterstock; 7T, © Orhan Cam/Shutterstock; 7M, © Sagittarius Pro/Shutterstock; 7B, © lazyllama/ Shutterstock; 9, © IPGGutenbergUKLtd/iStock; 11, © Orhan Cam/Shutterstock; 13, © Buyenlarge/Getty; 15, © ungvar/Shutterstock; 17, © Handout/Getty; 19, © Pool/Getty; 21, © Pool/Getty; 23, © Carl Iwasaki/ Getty; 25, © sirtravelalot/Shutterstock; 27, © ZUMA Press, Inc./Alamy; 28, © Orhan Cam/Shutterstock.

President: Jen Jenson
Director of Product Development: Spencer Brinker
Senior Editor: Allison Juda
Associate Editor: Charly Haley
Senior Designer: Colin O'Dea

Library of Congress Cataloging-in-Publication Data is available at www.loc.gov or upon request from the publisher.

ISBN: 978-1-63691-602-6 (hardcover)
ISBN: 978-1-63691-609-5 (paperback)
ISBN: 978-1-63691-616-3 (ebook)

For more information, write to Bearport Publishing, 5357 Penn Avenue South, Minneapolis, MN 55419. Printed in the United States of America.

Contents

Students Have a Say

Everyone in the United States has rights. This includes students. They don't lose the claim to be treated fairly when they walk into school. Students get to practice free speech and to **protest**. Who decided this? The United States Supreme Court did.

Students have spoken out about many things in schools. The Supreme Court said they could protest against the Vietnam War (1954–1975). Since then, students have stood against gun violence. They have supported LGBTQ rights.

Students have demanded changes to protect the planet.

The Judicial Branch

The Supreme Court is at the top of the **judicial** branch. This branch, or part of government, includes all the **federal** courts in the United States. The courts decide if people broke laws. They also say what laws mean.

The judicial branch is one of three branches in the U.S. government. The other two are the legislative branch and the executive branch. The legislative branch makes laws. The executive branch makes sure laws are carried out.

6

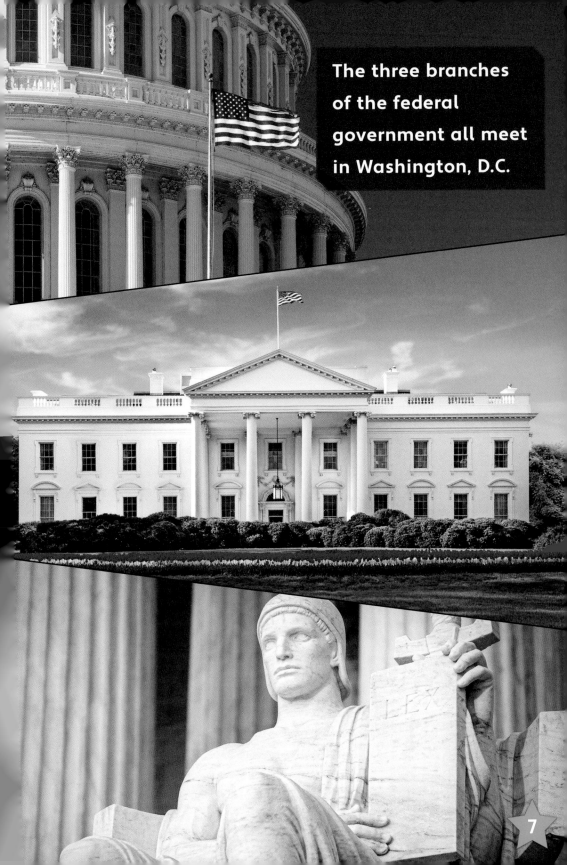

The three branches of the federal government all meet in Washington, D.C.

Level Up

The judicial branch is broken into three main levels. District courts, or **trial** courts, are the lowest level. Then, there are circuit courts. These are also called courts of **appeals**. People who want to challenge a district court's decision can appeal. They ask a circuit court to look at the case.

The higher the level of the court, the fewer there are. There are 94 district courts. Above those are only 13 courts of appeals.

Decisions in district courts come from a jury of people from the area.

Circuit courts can change the rulings, or decisions, of lower courts. But cases may still go on from there. The highest court in the system is the Supreme Court. It can make a change to all lower court decisions. There is only one Supreme Court at the top level.

Sometimes a higher court chooses not to take on a case. When that happens, the lower court's decision is final.

EQUAL·JUSTICE·UNDER·LAW

Landing at the Top

Cases usually go through at least one lower court before they make it to the Supreme Court. Just like when a case goes from a district to a circuit court, a case can be appealed to the Supreme Court. Very rarely, cases may go directly to the Supreme Court.

Most cases that go straight to the Supreme Court are about problems between state governments. They may be about who has the rights to places or things, such as sources of water.

The Supreme Court meets in the Supreme Court chambers.

13

Lower courts decide if laws are broken. But the Supreme Court is a little different. Its main role is to make sure court decisions are right. They look to the **Constitution** to do this. If laws or decisions go against rights from the Constitution, the Supreme Court can stop them.

Not every case makes it to the Supreme Court. The court is asked to look at more than 7,000 cases each year. But it only takes around 100 to 150 cases during that time.

The Constitution has guided the nation since 1789. The Supreme Court decides what its laws mean.

Justices

Courts are run by judges. The judges of the Supreme Court are called justices. There are nine justices on the court. All justices get a say on cases. But the chief justice leads the court. The other Supreme Court judges are called associate justices.

John G. Roberts Jr. is the current chief justice of the Supreme Court. He first took the job in 2005. Before that, he was a judge in different federal courts.

Chief Justice
John G. Roberts Jr.

How do judges make it to the Supreme Court? It all starts when the president picks a judge they want to join the court. Then, members of the legislative branch in the Senate vote. If most of the people in the Senate agree, the person becomes a new justice.

Justices stay on the court until they retire or die. A justice can also be removed from the court by impeachment. This may happen if a justice breaks the law.

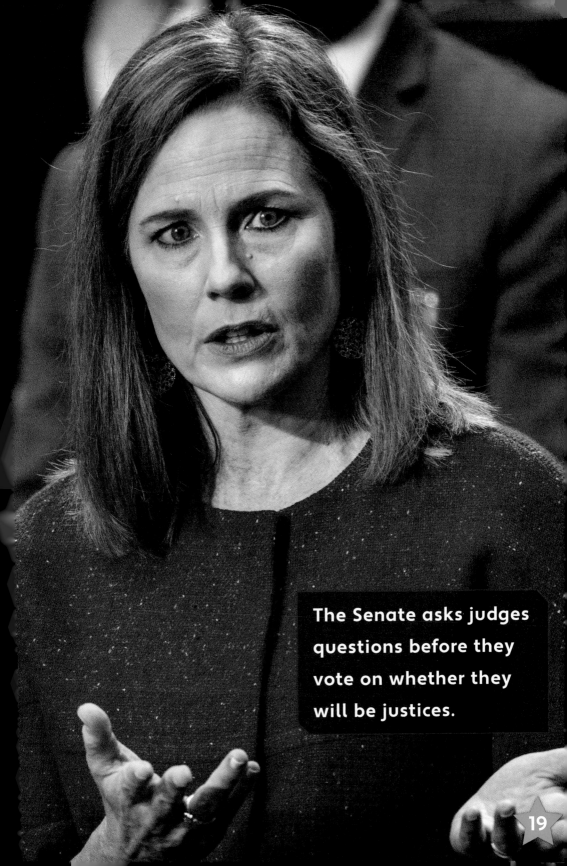

The Senate asks judges questions before they vote on whether they will be justices.

Court Cases

Cases at the Supreme Court start on paper. Each side writes about why they think they should win. Then, lawyers from both sides speak and the justices ask questions.

After that, the justices share their thoughts with one another. Then, they vote. The majority of votes decides the case.

A justice from the majority group writes an **opinion**. It tells why the decision was made. A justice who voted against the decision can also write an opinion. It says why they disagree.

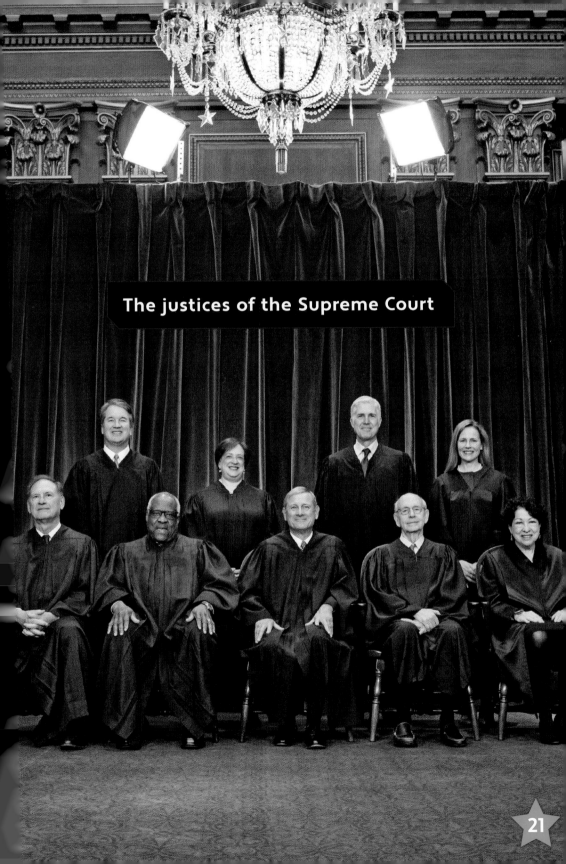

The justices of the Supreme Court

Big Changes

A Supreme Court decision doesn't just decide one case. It guides judges in lower courts, too. They use Supreme Court decisions to understand laws.

A decision in 1954 ended school **segregation**. It was called Brown v. Board of Education of Topeka. The Supreme Court said separate schools for white and Black students was illegal.

Segregation went against the 14th Amendment of the Constitution. This protects the rights of all people to be treated equally.

These families asked the Supreme Court to stop segregation in schools.

Other Supreme Court cases have made big changes as well. A Supreme Court decision says police need to tell you your rights before they question you. The reminder of rights is called the Miranda warnings after the 1966 Supreme Court case name.

The Miranda warnings protect people who may have broken the law. They do not have to speak if they don't want to.

Looking Back and Forward

The Supreme Court has changed in small ways over the years. In fact, even the number of justices has changed. Today, some think the number of justices should change again. We don't know the court's future. But we do know its decisions will affect Americans for years to come.

The number of justices on the court has changed six times. But since 1869, the court has had nine members.

People often come together outside the Supreme Court to speak their minds.

The Branches of Government

Legislative Branch	Executive Branch	Judicial Branch

Makes laws
Made up of the Senate and the House of Representatives

Carries out laws
Made up of the president, the vice president, and the president's cabinet

Says if laws are followed correctly
Made up of federal courts

The Supreme Court

The Supreme Court is the highest federal court. Nine justices work together to make sure the country's laws follow the Constitution.

SilverTips for SUCCESS

★ SilverTips for REVIEW

Review what you've learned. Use the text to help you.

Define key terms

appeals	justices
the Constitution	opinions
judicial branch	

Check for understanding

Name the levels of courts in the judicial branch. Where does the Supreme Court fall compared to other courts?

Describe the path a case may follow to make it to the Supreme Court.

What is the Supreme Court supposed to use to decide on cases?

Think deeper

How does the Supreme Court have an impact on your life? Name at least one example.

★ SilverTips on TEST-TAKING

★ **Make a study plan.** Ask your teacher what the test is going to cover. Then, set aside time to study a little bit every day.

★ **Read all the questions carefully.** Be sure you know what is being asked.

★ **Skip any questions** you don't know how to answer right away. Mark them and come back later if you have time.

Glossary

appeals requests to higher courts to review the decisions of lower courts

Constitution a statement of basic laws and principles for governing

executive relating to the branch of government that includes the president and vice president

federal having to do with the government of a nation

judicial related to the branch of government that includes courts and judges

legislative related to the branch of government with people who make laws

opinion a written explanation of why a decision was made according to laws or rules

protest to express disagreement with something; a demonstration against something is also called a protest

segregation the practice of separating people by groups, especially by race

trial an event that takes place in a court to decide if someone broke a law

Read More

Alexander, Vincent. *Judicial Branch (My Government).* Minneapolis: Jump! 2019.

Tolli, Jenna. *Inside the Supreme Court (Rosen Verified: U.S. Government).* New York: Rosen Publishing, 2021.

Wiseman, Blaine. *Supreme Court Justice (People in Our Government).* New York: Lightbox, 2020.

Learn More Online

1. Go to **www.factsurfer.com** or scan the QR code below.

2. Enter "**The Supreme Court**" into the search box.

3. Click on the cover of this book to see a list of websites.

Index

About the Author

Karen Latchana Kenney is a an author and editor. She lives in Minnetonka, MN.